THEOPHANIES

Printed in the United States

10 9 8 7 6 5 4 3 2 1

Alice James Books are published by Alice James Poetry Cooperative, Inc.

Alice James Books
Auburn Hall
60 Pineland Drive, Suite 206
New Gloucester, ME 04260
www.alicejamesbooks.org

Library of Congress Cataloging-in-Publication Data

Names: Ali, Sarah Ghazal, author.
Title: Theophanies / Sarah Ghazal Ali.
Description: New Gloucester, ME : Alice James Books, 2023.
Identifiers: LCCN 2023026663 (print) | LCCN 2023026664 (ebook) | ISBN 9781949944587 (trade paperback) | ISBN 9781949944310 (epub)
Subjects: LCGFT: Poetry.
Classification: LCC PS3601.L379 T47 2023 (print) | LCC PS3601.L379 (ebook) | DDC 813/.6--dc23/eng/20230803
LC record available at https://lccn.loc.gov/2023026663
LC ebook record available at https://lccn.loc.gov/2023026664

Alice James Books gratefully acknowledges support from individual donors, private foundations, and the National Endowment for the Arts.

Cover image: Dan Hillier (danhillier.com)

THEOPHANIES

SARAH GHAZAL ALI

Alice James Books
New Gloucester, Maine

CONTENTS

For the mother line

I gave you my name, Sarah. And it is a dead end road.

—Edmond Jabès

My Faith Gets Grime under Its Nails

١

قل—SAY, HE IS ALLAH, THE ONE

I confess to sleeping coiled on my night-
blue prayer mat

more often than standing bent in rukū.

Even when I posture piety
I blink steady, lashes keeping count of the hand-
knotted flowers fringing the rug

rather than God's pristine names.

The places I've prayed—elevators, Victoria's Secret
fitting room, the muck-slick meadow after rain—

will testify for or against me,
spilling through my Book of Deeds

in ink of blood or honeyed milk.

٢

قل—SAY, I SEEK REFUGE IN THE LORD OF MANKIND

My faith is feminine, breasted
and irregularly bleeding.

My faith gets grime under its nails,

unburies maybe-mothers
to suckle them sacred. I believe
what I can’t leave. I eat
hand-slaughtered beef

spared of pain, I laugh about the banyan tree

in Khyber chained by a drunk British officer
convinced it lurched toward him. I pull up a picture
online and show my mother the roses
planted neatly around it,

the rusted shackles no one dares remove.

قل—SAY, I SEEK REFUGE WITH THE LORD OF DAWN

Once a month blood roams

like mint over immaculate grass.

The adhan trills from my arboreal center.

Though excused, I wake
before the white thread of day-
break to open my window,

let the angels in

to spectate the ache
and erase a sin for every devoted cramp.
Lord, you pardon my pain.
Lord, I parable my name.
As best as I can

I am raising my hands—

٤

قل—SAY, O DISBELIEVERS

I read my char qul, cup my hands, and blow.
I misremember and enter with the wrong foot
first. A woman crowned

holy is a calamity worth repeating.

Eve languished
motherless among rotting cores,
the sweet stench of fruit flies

at last shown their purpose.

What wilt, what putrefaction

of her will to wonder. I wonder how
to hallow the women I've sprung from.
I haven't begot a thing but inherited
wounds, I can't help but bear

what barely belongs to me.

Sarai

A name is not unlike
a sexed body. Like mine,
it carries.

Is remembered most
for what it fails

to yield. A name
is a condition meant to last,

to outlast, as should a daughter, her mother
tongue.

I am but do not have
a daughter.

When I look in the lake,
who looks back

is a sister
self: O, little i—I

carry you as you
carry who I am waiting to be.

Theophanies

A pair of apples blistering under the sun—
my eyes have been so saturated.
Before dreamdeep, I start awake, overstimulated
by the stacking of my bones, their caress and jostle.

My granted days I could live or leave. Each loaned
breath I can—do—waste or wield, straining
for the *bell* in *belief*. How an arrow flees limb to pierce.
How a pen bleeds to grant shape to speech.

In each instance of angels' descent,
they soothe: *Do not fear*, O Hajar, Maryam,
vesseled thee. Or is it awe that clamors the flesh?
A raptor's lean shadow for a flash

obliterating the high-noon sun: may it be
done to me so clearly. Like sirens. Like chimes.

Ghazal Ghazal

My people are lovers of the sher, qasida, ghazal.
My people memorize the Qur'an & recite the ghazal.

My god elicits trust through aqsam, oath after oath.
My people sing, *Don't insist on leaving tonight*, Farida's ghazal.

My people must include my father, his voice swinging from baritone to bellow.
Did my god not make his mouth, aural imprint of every sung ghazal?

My people say I am a morsel of their great, green liver. My people love first
like vultures, then martyrs. Death the sprawling shadow behind each sunlit ghazal.

My people are bordered. My people are borderless. My god swears
by the fig, the olive, the brightest star, the prophet who penned no ghazal.

My father practiced his english with me. I want to blame him.
My voice void of, my throat hostile to ghazals.

My father uncovered my hair. I want to blame him.
My prayers might never reach my god, nor my entreating ghazals.

Am I of my people? Do I please my lord?
My hair was bared, but someone veiled named me Ghazal.

Temporal

At five, my father shows me a color-
coded model of the brain. We take it

apart together, piece by heavy
plastic piece. Blue: temporal

lobe. Burrowed within, a red bean:
the amygdala. *Like a seed?*

Yes, he laughs, *where feelings bud.*
I picture currant anger, pleasure amassing

in brick and berry, and fear as a clotting kind
of dark: the first prick of blood on a thumb.

I unlimb my dolls, braid and section
their stiff hair. I scratch

their painted eyes,
chide them for their lack of

anything occipital (I've seen it, pried open
the skulls, found them

empty). I wish I could be
taken apart. Thank what keeps me

alive inside. *Amygdala*
from *almond*, the precise shape

of our eyes, mine and his
identical but for his laugh lines.

To live is to see but the walls of my body,
flesh the furthest point from the formless

God my father never joins me
in believing. Each spring he tends fervently

his garden, coaxes to life new green.
Genesis splits the earth anew.

Decreed in old age to bear a son,
my namesake trusted the parts

she couldn't see, the buds God insisted
were there, whole nations within her.

From beyond scripture,
she returns to crawl

through my throat. Her involuntary sound
a revelation: *I'm frightened. I'm awestruck.*

She lingers in the periphery,
shaded behind doors. Faith a legacy

of echoes—every echo
a reflection of voice. I still hear her

laughter—what I know is the brain's
doing. What I believe bewilders me.

Annunciation

My pillaged body
is not as interesting
as my virginal sister's,
I know. Your books
efface me, dismiss me
as naturally lacking.
So my hair has long
since grayed, cropped
short, held back
under a matronly veil.
I sent my husband to bed
another woman—I'm nobler
for it. I allowed a slight
to get the ball rolling.
By moonlight I grieved
the perpetual
blood marbling red
and black down my thighs.
They visited me first,
you know. God
and two angels came
with glad tidings,
announced I would flower
with a boy. But
all you remember

is what came next:
I hung my head and laughed.
When God at last
conferred my body
with fruit, the angels
raised their yellow wings.
They broke bread.
I listened until I heard
a great humming.
A child, a ripe boy
I would mother. The hive
coming to me
after all I'd done—
what else inside
to offer at the moment
of absolution but a flash
of sound? I knew
I wasn't favored
but damned. My whole
long life I'd been groomed
to unfurl for the coming
of bees. I knew
when I passed, he
would go back to her
and you to your Mater Dei,
your lily among thorns.
After all this, knowing
I'd be written over,
a vessel forgettable

but for a moment of sonic
lapse, tell me—
what would you have done?

Magdalene

To tell it once is not enough.
—Emily Skaja

God made laughter for the incredulous third.
We cover our mouths, abashed to echo her.

We bleed as penance for the curious first. When we don't,
we dread the burden borne by the immaculate second.

I submitted once, faithfully, and it was years
before I bloated with shame. He touched my hair with unsullied hands.

My hair that molted under cover of moonlight.
On a dewing street I stood bare and pinned by desire.

On a street pinnate with walnut I yielded. What else?
Doesn't *Islam* mean *submission*? The subordinate *to God*

conveniently elided. O seraphim reading over my shoulder,
dutiful scribes, again just for you: I submitted faithfully to a man.

What else? More—I was confounded by an opulent voice.
He loved to drawl my name, lilting into the *ah*

like it was an exclamation. He spoke my name and made me
a performance—a public, deviating miracle.

In our town by the sea, we walked our own procession,
        the last two leaves clinging to a dead stalk.

I'll mark this obscene. I'll demean
        the ragged shore we once deemed holy.

If God willed, I'd live wholly
        without want. I'd kneel and with my hair dry His feet.

Motherhood 1999

That year my mother made herself tall
with routine, nutrifying
my body, my bell inclined to bloat

empty and ringing. Today my own
cool fingers button tight against throat,
its silence, years of my mouth's refusal,

but that spring she beseeched tirelessly
my stone teeth. In anger she stretched
inches red and hoisted me up

onto the kitchen windowsill overlooking the grass
below. My mother leaned close, commanded: *Swallow*
or be swallowed by the lawn. I looked at her.

Who could save me from a love that forced me full?

First triumph of her spine, the only daughter
followed by son and son. From her palm she sliced
pieces, and I balled each bite in my cheek.

Long Island, where I can't recall a father
but in photographs, where aunts unfurled fingers
to catch all I spat. We slept under stars

of artificial green, my mother's hand pressing hymns
against my back. Waiting now for spring, I grow thin
with the day's light. Her voice through the phone

is rising heat, pushing me closer to the birds.
I boil rice. Measure years into jars.
Run a finger over each rim until it sings.

Whittled down to pocket, I've kept careful proportion
to the hands I fell through. Height a matter
of angle—whether I lean into a sound or away.

Spectacle

The doctor uses a mirror to see
inside me. His speculum yawns

but my mouths clench
and I am disciplined with pain.

An exercise in elision:

Ibrahim and his blade,
one son offered or the other.

Hajar consoled Sarah consoled Hajar.
Bystanders squint with both eyes.

When labor afflicts my abdomen,
they'll check to see if I'm effaced,

if my cervix is thin,
ripe enough to leak fresh life.

When a father approaches a mother,
he forgets to check the door

ajar and shading a watchful girl
who sees him raise his blade

of a hand—its straight and narrow path.
Who consoled Hajar consoled who?

The wick of tonight's sandalwood candle
without flinching shoulders a flame.

Matrilineage [Umbilicus]

the first inheritance   a puncture wound:

where you detach from   your mother

an undug grave   call it provenance

in one language named   *life source* حواء

eve. *the period preceding*   some say *wife/mother of [ ]*

but origin can't be   tethered to consequence

an oculus   doomed to gape before a mirror

my abdomen rounded   a line appeared

from navel to sex   linea nigra

text appeared   ا   the first letter

abjad   inferred,   ا

mammalian   I, matriline

I did not want this   look how

it appeared I multiplied

from figment I bore

witness: your body

Roadkill Elegy

In good towns, good houses mourn what dies
outside by closing windows.

Bullfrog caught in a mower black-red. Driveway
chalk gray-red. Tire-tracked doe red-red.

Under a sycamore my throat whirls from pity
to nausea. The suburban sky does nothing, sees less.

Another small chest deflates at the edge of my vision
before gas tank heaves and gut tries to follow.

The angel on my left shoulder finds something
of interest in the windshield blur of road then red,

body then blood. He bites my ear and pulls
hard my lashes. *Look,* he insists, *where I point.*

Where shells split. Where color leaks. *Look,*
he demands. My own palms spangled with crime.

He walks across my blades and drags a fleshy bone
behind him. In lurid dreams I resurrect them all,

or they refuse to leave, guilt dressed as grace.

A frog or my fingers, the blade always a blade.

In good towns, good children collapse
snake holes, heel away ant hills for sport.

Above us, a gray-necked warbler shrieks and shrieks
a humdrum dirge for these ordinary deaths.

I drive on, bound by time. He sings, knitted
to his perch on a telephone wire, eyes

fixed to each body I blur past, flaring
car after car like poppies on pool water, red.

Cicatrix

Like a good womb

I pad my walls with blood.

The wisps of hair

traipsing north from my navel

I privately christen

my flesh-trenched Radcliffe Line.

This doltish name

a dilution of land—*red cliff*

as in, precipice

as in, imperial crag.

Like a good woman

I wound myself first.

Like a good wound

I laugh until my mouth rips.

Every August

my chest bloats lucent.

Like clockwork

I suffer the seductions of partition

a bright nail

dragging still-warm flesh

into the lacuna

into an inflamed century

of new nations

teetering on the bluff of stolen exaltations.

Story of the Cranes

١

A young girl with a face full of eyes asks her baba,

Baba, do you know
everything?

Baba tells her he knows everything.

Through seeping eyes, lies appear
feathered with truth.

She offers him a red book
from the shelf with another question.

Baba tells her *The Satanic Verses* is a secret God
kept from us, stories Shaytan wasn't allowed to share,
Poor Shaytan.

Shouldn't he get to tell his side of things?

Baba points out the window.
Shaytan wants us to worship the birds.

Baba knows cranes fly with necks elongated.

That there were three beautiful and beloved long ago.
He knows them in Farsi, in Urdu.

But in Arabic—*al-Gharaniq* الغرانيق
This she learned on her own.

Baba installs a birdbath.
So the cranes might bless us with their presence!

Baba goes bird-watching.
God is here, around us, not above!

At the park, her eyes shutter if Baba comes too close.
He always pushes the swing too high.

٢

Birds flood my dreams,
fill the night and cut me.

I memorized the names of every human
bone, shoulder to finger, to stay awake.
Despite my best efforts, I'd drift off, always
waking with shoulders sore, phantom

pain reminding me what my body was not
made for.

What was my body made for?

٣

Today, two colorless birds drag
their shadows across the grass.

I imagine looping wire thread around their bodies,
tossing them into the air like broken kites.
It's too easy to be cruel now.

I demonstrate to the creatures in audience
my full and human length. How high
I can stretch, arms breaching their sky.

٤

God addresses the three cranes by name,
devotes two of sixty-two verses to this end.

I imagine the young girl in audience as the Prophet
stands to echo this surah to a crowd.

I see her child eyes,
how easily they reveal their want.

I learned on my own
that when he finished speaking,
believers and nonbelievers alike fell to their knees,

so affected were they by the answer
to questions no one knew to ask.

I see her falling with the best of them, devotion rippling
across her face.

ه

In the mirror, the wrong eyes run down my face.

Baba, do you know
everything?

Baba smiles
and shows me his long neck.

Aurat

By the time the angels intervened
the ache had long fled the fields,

irretrievable by then,
and what it took from me was gone.

There were no letters left
to taste in the chosen language of God

and only english was left to me,
only english absolved me

of what was coaxed from my lap
while I looked

away and through the window open
like an eye over the bed.

Desire made a door of me
and I kept it ajar.

In my mother's house I revert to her
body's bloom. In her language

a woman is what she shrouds, skin paling
under cloth, a chamber of grit and two-

lipped rooms. In the language of revelation
I'm told this word is a slur, means *defective*

or *deficient.* From navel to knee, it marks me
a garden to be raked clean by a husband.

Vulnerable is a body beneath
a body beneath a shared gray sheet.

It was April, evening,
one star glinting in the maw.

I lay still.
I didn't bleed.

Litany of al-Bayt

Some mornings blood falls
it hardly bears repeating—and yet

and each house presupposes a master
and each womb obtrudes a stain
and each time, God spoke to loosely defined sons
said *Purify my house for those who circle it*
said *Build the house*
and *Raise the foundations of the house*
and *Found the faith of the house*
and *Ask for the house*
to be accepted

and so Ibrahim and Isma'īl [a father and one of two sons]
raised it stone by black stone
and so honored the Divine ask

and each house presupposes a keeper
and the house spoke *Ibrahim is the keeper of my rooms*
said *I am the direction for your canonical prostrations*
said *I am the six-faced heart of the one God*

and each woman obtrudes with her tongue
and each time a woman spoke [somewhere Sarah, elsewhere Hajar]
to father and son

and asked *Who is your origin?*

asked *Who barrows your flesh from day to month?*

asked *Who ordains a man born of me*

while my likeness bears a stone?

and the men laughed

and the House laughed

and the Divine spoke *No*

a stone isn't borne

it falls

and from it seeps water

like tears from an eye

Tumulus

and weren't we all
once slick
girls in the bath, knees
to chest, thinking
of Maryam, effigy
of maidenhood?
hunched and afraid
drawn to the inconceivable
latch of her miracle,
the feat of our own
withholding cisterns.
if the flood came
we all swore we would
again be good, better
even. if we were spared,
we would harken back,
remember God
could stitch life
through a grave. now,
carmine weaving between
my ankles days later
than expected, I recall
a friend who refused
to let a man touch her
before they wed, who feared

God would curse her
with a suckling
of packed sediment,
dead weight in her tomb.
but punishment must be
ancillary to mercy, a scar
rewritten as a sign,
something before
which we cower—no,
marvel. O Maryam,
is birth not its own
inhumation,
did your child not emerge
perfectly alive
and written to die?

Self-Portrait as Epiphany

I thought myself
 a child. The river revealed me

a basket. Within, a doomed girl. Grew
 and groomed. When came the bush,

I knew to burn. To shear errant tongues
 probing the cage.

Mother sang of deliverance. Father prayed
 for a son. I revised myself

a daughter. Renounced duty. Rolled
 stones down my throat.

In a dream, the angel reveals me a book.
 I learn myself grime

among false gods. Unashamed
 I cramp. Between my legs

a clot. From a clot
 I'll make men. Hollow

myself holy.

Nothing laughs like me.

Brittle, brutish—a woman
baring her teeth.

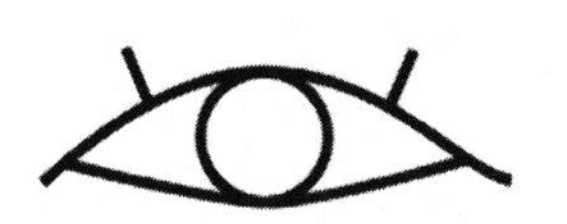

Parable of Flies

I heard them, wings beating
a din beyond the thistle, pilgrims
beckoned by the promise of carrion.

Lured by the lurid, I followed
their song off the path, turned my back
to the lake. Angels fled the quarry,

thirst a blight in their wake. The flies,
their mouths roved like dogs
the breast of a sundered wren,

chest wide as a lens, steady
spectator of its own death.
This is an economy

of asylum. Ruddy flesh calls,
Come and brutes abound,
haloing their openhanded new home.

I'm divining my body a dirtied domestic.
When it rains, devotion is the womb
I've hollowed to keep desire dry.

Ghazal on the Day of

Like God, I'll create in my image. Go on, pass judgment
—like I'm not already waiting for judgment,

like I don't tease, don't taunt to turn His eye my way.
Like I'm not expiring, short-sticked by a judgment

foretold in unteachable, spiraling math. Each sky's
bloated yolk barrels toward the day of judgment.

Seeded, I take seeds to stifle my soil's waiting green.
I liken my name to apology. I wield judgment

like a snapped beak and shovel night from my abdomen.
Are you watching, O corkscrew calamity, O decree,

O closer than jugular? Come for this constellating mess.
I'm sorry for laughing, O giver, not for taking, so judge.

Daughter

Too stubborn
to supplicate, I bend for luster

not love. For absolution, I break my bones,
soften gristle with what teeth remain.

Mine an umbilical affliction without cure.
Do you think I asked to eavesdrop

through inherited eyes?
Recite to me a single memory not manufactured.

Even a mother is myth, fabling
to survive a marriage   miscarriage   man.

Call me a reed. Voices lake
behind my eyes.

The rims of wounds have wounds
as well. I have a theory about mirrors

that I won't risk repeating.
The women who made me already know.

Le viol, René Magritte, 1934

I have seen a gecko tongue his lidless eye,
head still, watching for movement,
jaw hinging open almost imperceptibly
in the modulating heat of midday.
I have seen his throat ripple as he begins
to chirp proprietarily, then flee—no,
chase—another, evidently female,
her body going slack, easily acquiescing to his.

And I have seen a plum pucker in a man's
tight grip, split sudden without protest
on the banks of the Sambre, vermilion
sluicing his arm. Next to him a woman,
obedient window, taught to permit
the outside to participate. I have seen
him stain all but her face—
I have seen her bruiseless face.

I have seen pockets fill with stones, blue
mouths agape in the black depths of this river.
I have watched crimes of looking blur
into taking. I have been, I have been
and not put up a fight—
a stone chosen for its smoothness

then hurled against the skin of the sea.

Matrilineage [Parthenogenesis]

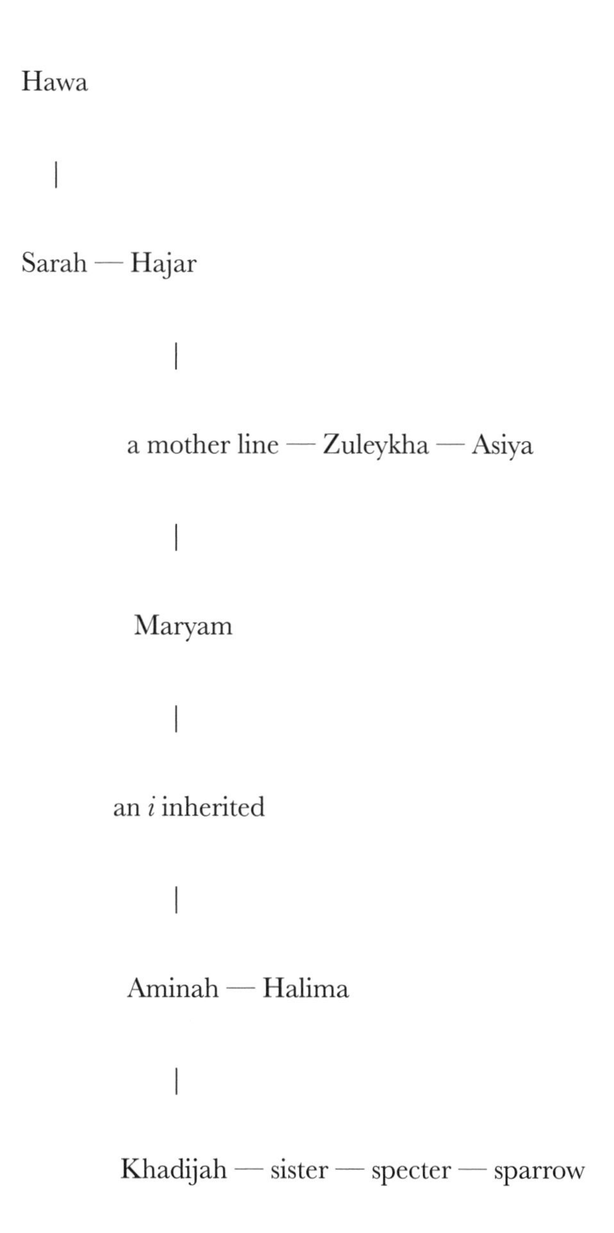

|

Fatima

|

a thrashing of wings

|

Sarwari

|

my mother: *great* — sister: *phoenix* — sister: *pearl*

|

I — O eye — O eyed —

Shirk

Years after our end, I looked up
the meaning of his name: *enveloping sky*.
In the Qur'an, the sky is at one point
cloth tented over bare dirt,
at another a ceiling vaulting
the tender bed of the earth
from comets or acid rain,
solar flares, alluring guests.
And He restrains the sky from falling on
a girl, bright-haired and eager to sweat
in a non-God's bed. *unless*
by His permission. He asked
before entering, and I gave
permission. To say otherwise
a lie, though one God allows
with private remorse, as in, *bitten*
again, a morsel of flesh ripped
from me. Ichor dewing
at the lip of a wound: juice
from the first apple slicking the mouth
of the first man. I was penitent,
but not before he entered again
and again, the Lord

I briefly believed, his body
above me an eclipse,
a spectacle I'd been
warned not to watch.

Partition Ghazal

Everyone carries his address in his pocket
so that at least his body will reach home.
—Agha Shahid Ali

There from once-claimed land buds a sudden country.
Unsurprising, as every tale is the tale of your country.

A man traces his lazy finger down a map, one hand
perforating a body—pulling from it a country.

Which do you claim? Where are you unseen
among the people of this or that country?

Your father's father watches from the walls,
a partridge falling from its sky of no country.

He fell silent and bitter, hastily married off to heal
the rift with the peculiar balm of a woman's country.

and Musa parted—but only sea. This chasm light seeps
through, this sunless path to a discarnate country.

And your father's mother? Too young to tend a land-
less man with no allegiance to her, only his lost country.

Blasphemous how one begets many. Father, father, daughter.
And your mother? Miraculous origin, the one natural country.

When they ask, Ghazal, if you anger, recite again: men
always flee for the anthem of a new country.

The Ideal

Mother bursts with child without
bleeding. Her attenuated wrists bear heavy

bangles, coupled and gold, embracing
a tasteful watch she doesn't need

to check. Her hair a sheathed black,
never mottling, even under glare

of sun. Her skin pristine, unrippled by sin
or prior loss. In a thermal scan she appears

a chilled blue, her depths placid.
She doesn't complain in heat or unnatural

shafts of light, even when
startled by a winged apparition.

She is kind to strangers on the bus.
She offers gum and sunscreen.

In her dreams, visions of the impossible
sons, fathers of faiths. A first and singular

child of some hearsay divine.
When the command comes, the ideal

drops her groceries. Without shame
she lifts her dress and leans back on her haunches.

She waits for salvation to fall and it does,
colostrum seeping—the opaline hue of it

sears her bare hands.

Litany with Hair

and God said *veil*
    said *pull it over your breast*

and mama said *I miss it long*
    said *wish you can grow it back*

and baba said *not explicit*
    said *where does it say to?*

and God said *O believing men restrain your eyes*

and mama said to a man *you hypocrite lower your dirty eyes*

and God said *O believing women*
    said *this is purer for you*
    said *I am aware of all you do*

and mama said *wish mine grew like yours*

and baba said *it hides you*
    said *makes you ugly*
    said *not my daughter*
    said *not in my house*
    said *not anymore*

and mama said *yes, ugly*
said *[nothing for days]*

and God said *do not substitute what is bad for what is good*

and mama said *so thick so beautiful*

and God said *you dislike a thing and I have placed good in it*

and baba said *not my daughter*
said *brainwashed*

and I said—
but who heard?

Daughter Triptych

So surely with hardship comes ease.
Surely, with hardship comes ease.
—Qur'an 94:5-6

١

After my first time, I dreamed of abortions. Some might have been mine: oblong pink pills, a curved door handle, wire hanger, unripe papaya. One night, I looked out from the eyes of Maryam. A sharpened stake in our hand. Back against a date palm, no wail escaping our lips, no surveilling angel to interfere. Then I was elsewhere, watching Sarah, aged and exhausted. Her fingers pressed light against that slightest bulge. Her fingers curled. Her fingers pressing pressing pushing pummeling pounding. Her eyes closed. *Not now not now not now* then finally, her body acquiescing. A fate for daughters exacted upon sons. In sleep, I cramp. I cradle the part of me that begs to bud. I wonder what might have happened—not if God had left us alone, but if we refused what He offered.

٢

Shukr karo, uncle says,
they used to bury daughters alive.

Daughter to sister to wife to mother, my mother
never slept alone. The first room of her own

her grave. After her first time, her first
floret a daughter.

The Prophet said, *If you have daughters*
and do not bury them, or slight them, or prefer
your sons to them, they will be a shield
for you on the day of judgment.

Uncle says, *A shame—with daughters come*
hardship. To Uncle she serves tea, nods.

I am not enough to prove otherwise.

٣

A man came to see the Prophet and asked,
O Messenger! Who among people is most deserving of good treatment?

The Prophet said, *Your mother.*
The man asked, *After her?*
The Prophet said, *Your mother.*
The man asked, *And then?*
The Prophet again replied, *Your mother.*
The man asked, *Then who?* And
the Prophet said, *Your father.*

A girl dreamed she stood before God so asked,
O Lord! And if my father mistreats my mother?

Apotheosis

Listen—if I've learned anything from men,
it's that their tongues are bare
and motherless, lapping the breast of brawn
they mistake for a masculine God.

Too young, I've earned the word *behead*
in my mother tongue— سر قلم کرنا
How young? She, named for light, was twenty-seven.
My hunger for fresh language carries me
closer to violent shores, gravel voices.

Once before Fajr I cracked a date pit between
my teeth, tilted the sharp half into a lover's mouth.
I tested the crimson I was sure seethed beneath
his, every man's, skin. *You're like a furnace,*
he whispered, dry against my sweat-laced back.

It's true I dream of hands
hot around my throat, the finger marks
I saw fading grime-green on [   ]'s.
No one has blued me, but still I wake
afraid, keening until the complex dogs bark back.

How to fathom it, my grandfather alive now
longer than our new-bloom nation. پاک means *pure.*

Land of the Pious, pigless and pissed-upon. Partition
a moment un-begun, a dirge without end.
I sing its songs. I marry its men. I, like my mother,

wait to be bent to better congruities.
اسلام means *submission.* Oh, I submit to any
merciful creature, angle ready to deify
the Eden beneath any child-swollen feet.

My faith in God was inevitable as an oil spill,
my childhood slick with sky-bound yammering,
questions and confessions hurled against the slapbrush ceiling.
In '47 did they say بِسمِ الله before un-bloating
wombs, lifting the never-born like alms to the All-Seeing?

I know nothing of God's plan or the invasive empires
of devotion, gardens I waste away wanting.
I fell heir to my father's hands, anguish, eyes—
the crimes of man beget the crimes of man.

Self-Portrait as Mouthpiece of God

In most versions I am
impossible—

flesh immolated by the hot voice
of a calling angel,

not sybil, never
a throat for any wise man or lord's speech,

though I too was once congealed
blood, a mere clot,

and I too became
a clump of sinew, then grew

a body of man though I am
no man nor prophet,

not an oracle nor beautiful
enough to tongue a syllable of revelation.

My hair is palmed and pulled,
my form lithe, obedient and so

kept vacant. I heed all commands.

I bear the brunt, someday
even a child and once I'm a mother

paradise will beckon from beneath
my ordinary feet.

No, not mouthpiece, but gaping
cervix, marrow blown from the concave

neck of a bone, and still
a message worth hearing.

Mother of Nations

By now it's almost boring: the peal
of Sarah's bewildered laugh.
The sidelined matriarch, barren
until she wasn't. I pretend

not to hear Sarah's bewildered laugh.
How does a barren tomb sound? Waiting
until she wasn't. I pretend to be honeycomb
sucked clean, scraped raw.

The sound of a barren tomb: waiting
each month for the inevitable wilt
of a cervix sucked clean, scraped raw.
Hajar had it easy—until she didn't—

sprouting, spared the inevitable monthly wilt.
Sarah's throat plumed right in God's face.
Hajar had the easy job until she didn't.
But enough. It's boring—watching faith peel.

Failed Ghazal for *Log Kya Kahenge*

Each pearl strung on a necklace collides with its neighbor.
When [   ] jumped from the window, did they see? The neighbors?

Flower flower flower flower
Today for the sake of all the dead Burst into flower.

—Muriel Rukeyser

O Gabriel

O umbilical mesh
apogee of angels
O ungendered & sex-
less courier
O jagged nail
fattening on His finger
O arch
and archive O bush
ablaze O throat   O throat
O uterine throat
O mediary of Mary
of Musa O pillar of cloud
O brute force O being
unborn yet sent to make me
see O brilliant light
O blotting dark—

God tugs at whim your corded tongue

so tilt an ear and shade me

with your heel break open
a fount as you did for my sister

all my rooms are greening in wait

pull back my falling shroud
see how well I bear the burden

a child

come sigh
for once in me

The Guest

I heard his knock in the corridors of sleep
and woke to let him in.

Imagine my heart in my feet
as I stepped out of bed and over a snake

that darted away so fast I doubted my eyes,
whether it really grazed my ankle

or if my sight convinced me
of some artificial touch—

all the dramatics of a retina
eager to spin brightness from a long night.

I am trying not to conflate
snakes with the first garden,

trying not to fixate on capacity,
on travelers morphing into conquerors

but patterns becoming means
for celestial navigation,

trying to focus on the guest, patient,
waiting behind a door.

The Bedouins dubbed him
Tariq—a morning star
mapping the sand of a dream.

There was a room—I touched its walls.
A figure—his knock rustled behind my eyes.

There was a diaphanous scene leaking
through the gap under my door.

I blamed the trees for their wood, I wondered
if he was tired from walking. If the grass

constellated beneath him. If his eyes darkened
with the night. I press hard against mine.

Magdalene Diptych

after George de la Tour's Magdalene at a Mirror

If what I saw befell your sight
the epiphany would stream down
your face, an exodus
of melting, retinal butter.

So I haven't washed in days.
What do you know of a spectator's plight?

They tell me in that garden
he saw every imminent sin.
So he must have known, before
I did, all you would come to think of me.

I have no interest in the aviary
you keep of my names. The one bright
gift of my life is that I was
witnessed. The only thing
God asks of me is to bear it.

The one bright gift of my life is that I was

witnessed. Before I could be seen

I learned touch. My fingers,

your skull. In my hands now

you are nothing but bone,

alabaster marked for carving.

The penultimate Prophet, plucked

back by the exacting hand of our child-

less God—The Sustainer

places before me this herald of rot.

Often I confuse *theophany* and *theophagy*.

How a flame helps you see me in this curated room.

How when you carry on, tired of looking,

it licks then swallows me whole.

Eid al-Adha

That you have already killed a blindfolded goat,
stroked its fur as it bled against your jeans.

Were I to touch warm blood,
eyes closed, I'd think it my own.

Your dry hand over mine, urging me
to follow my dreams, my throat

hitching charily around the pill
of permission.

A tale as reliant on who tells as who listens,
on the temperament attributed

to each version's God. One version:
Ibrahim was commanded, so obliged,

so rewarded with the goat,
a substitute sacrifice.

Another: he woke from a dream,
divined it a sign. I don't claim

to know which son, but believe he nodded,
insisted, *You must.* His eyes closed.

His hand tightening over his father's.
Pulling the blade toward himself.

Must I keep seeing. These rites
my father forbade. The dream roiling

turbid through me, through me
a dream calving limbs, speaking.

That you sat holding its cooling body,
whispering ninety-nine names to soothe

until it stilled. The angle of the knife capable
of precluding pain. That I believe this,

and you, holding close
the exegeses of fallible men.

Fatal Music

The leaves of the fig tree are lobed and bright. In another country, they shade me before I learn to register them. Faith follows me like this. Never heavy, and whole with or without me. At dusk, I walk through an orchard and choir its fruit into the basin I make of my blouse.

I love most that object which evokes another. How the split fig on my tongue leaks honey, gummy resin of eternal rivers.

In the other country, I begin to impersonate a more desirable self: penumbra. From mosque to mosque I carry a book of elegies. A purple shawl I pull shyly over my hair. *What is it you urgently ask for if not transformation?* How hungry my gaze is to swell, but the angels are indifferent to me.

In home videos, my child self presses her face to the camera and asks, over and over, *Are you looking at me?* Seeing her face erodes something in mine, though I've finally grown into her eyes.

The angels elsewhere tune their instruments, polish their preludes. What they blow with their breath will make a song of death.

For the Trumpet shall be blown, and whosoever is in the heavens and whosoever is in the earth shall swoon, save whom God wills. Then it shall be blown again, and lo, they shall stand, beholding.
—Qur'an 39:68

An orchestra, then, a cataclysm that tunnels through the ears, and I still foolishly beholden to the sugar of each sclera.

Once, a winged thing pressed hot coal to Isaiah's lips. Once, a swarm of feathers shielded the someday-Prophet from view as hands pulled apart each rib, fished out his heart, and polished it.

Iqra, Qul, *read, say*—but I am stubborn, red-eyed, waiting for a different imperative. So much could lie beyond the lattice of this language that I finger but cannot unlatch. How full a tender fig in my palm before I've bitten it. How sweet the fruit of a soil I was born beginning to leave.

When Nabra Hassanen Wakes Up in Jannah

She will peer at the back of her hands
now translucent with the bluish
quality of a body observed underwater.
Nabra Hassanen will see the blood
swirling just beneath her skin
and it will be a sweetness to her eyes.
Nabra Hassanen will be surrounded
by the trees she spent a brief lifetime
earning—*Glory be to Allah*—
do they still accumulate after death,
after the new and final beginning?
All praise is to Allah—Nabra Hassanen
will test these words and all others,
look around for a sudden spurting
of limbs and leaves and hum with delight
when her gaze is granted, at last,
immediate reward. There will be
no need for hijab here, no
men with appraising eyes, no
reason to ever again face rage.
Nabra Hassanen will walk
and reach for fruit, remembering
her mother, all those years
knifing berries into ordinary bowls.

Nabra Hassanen will see again
her mother's two hands pulling apart
a pomegranate, teaching her
that each orb houses one
blessed seed from a tree in Jannah.
Nabra Hassanen will hope to find her
beyond these trees among others
resting in the sweet shade of mercy.
Nabra Hassanen will be scared
that the miracle might end,
that the garden might sense her
boundless human wants.
Nabra Hassanen will float along, buoyed
by the thousands, still earthbound,
who bent in congregation at her janazah.
God is greater, she will laugh.
Nabra Hassanen will never be asked again
to qualify, to answer, *Than what?* Nor
will she remember how she arrived—

Matrilineage [Recovered]

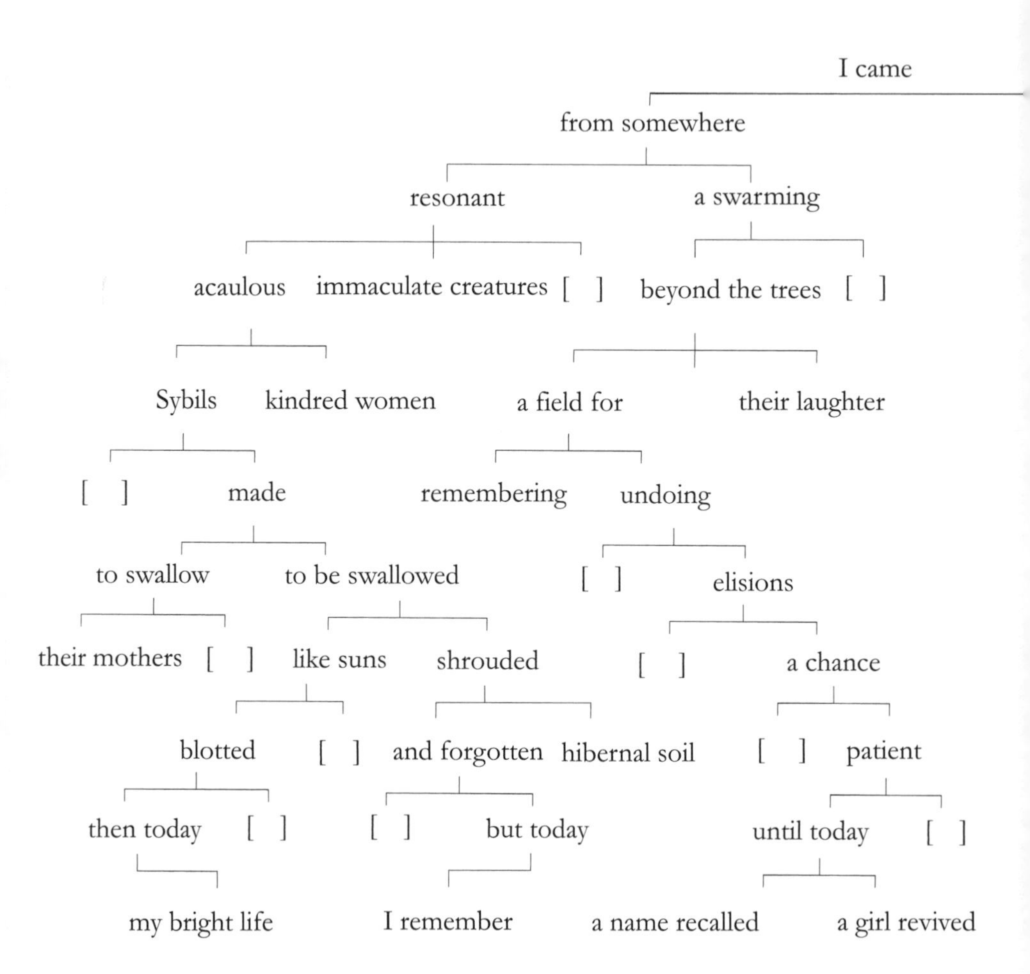

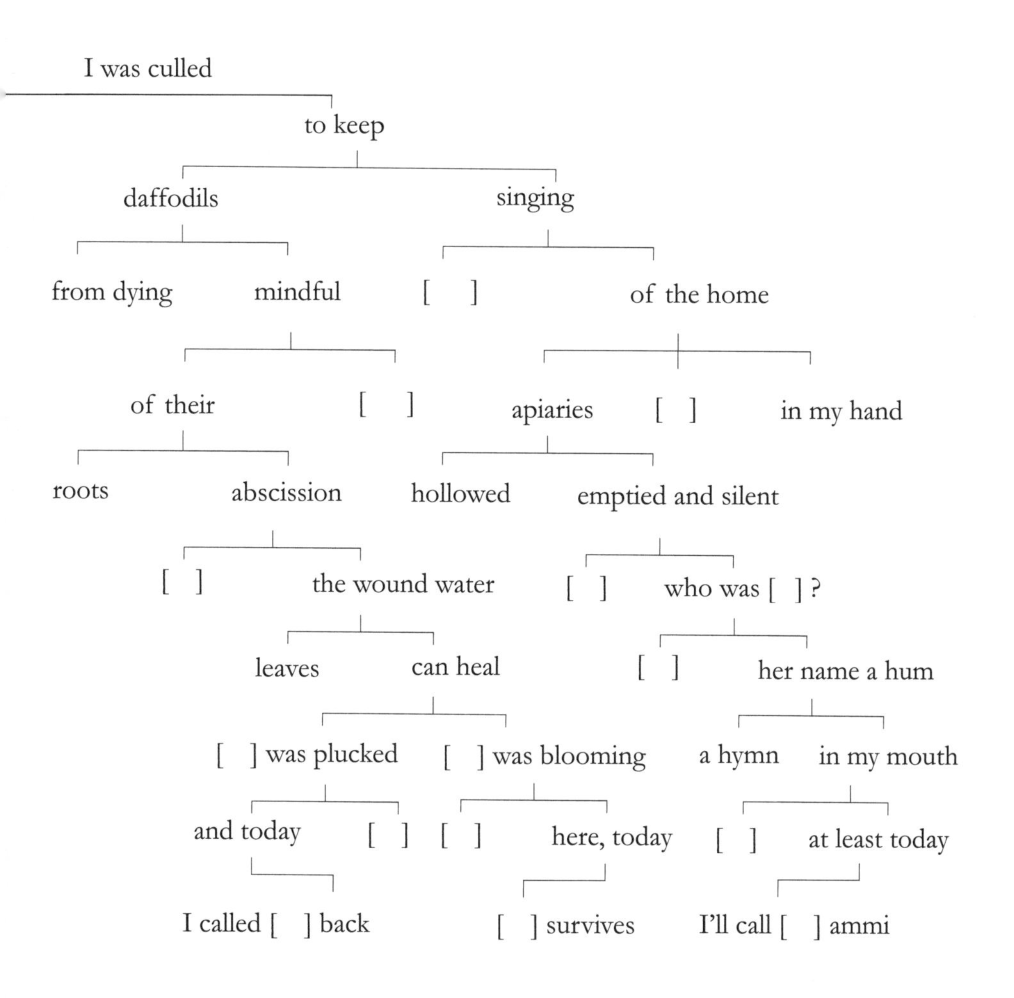
I was culled
to keep
daffodils
singing
from dying
mindful
[ ]
of the home
of their
[ ]
apiaries
[ ]
in my hand
roots
abscission
hollowed
emptied and silent
[ ]
the wound water
[ ]
who was [ ] ?
leaves
can heal
[ ]
her name a hum
[ ] was plucked
[ ] was blooming
a hymn
in my mouth
and today
[ ]
[ ]
here, today
[ ]
at least today
I called [ ] back
[ ] survives
I'll call [ ] ammi

February Augury

Yulan magnolias blossom first
as birds

little feathered fists
I admit to

imagining could harm me,
extending barefaced

from trees, the known
homes of jinn

I'm told. The night deepens and
locusts halo my head

or don't. Believe me
I barely believe

the heralds I've seen, the mirror
windowed if I stare

a beat too long, my face refracting
others, foremothers,

my beloved's hands rising
in supplication under winter

rain, stopping after spotting
the dead sparrow by the door

bent like a comma—
as if asking him

to pause, or telling me
to wait.

Theophanies

If nothing else, at least this clemency: two whorls
in each face, round pistils burrowed and searching.
Tariq asks what I saw in my sleep. I weave a sweet

lie about my mother's pomegranates, the kitchen
tiles we bloodied searching for the seed in each
rumored to belong to a mirror tree in paradise.

The truth: a girl with melting eyes
who holds my gaze all night, vitreous rivers
gushing down our faces until one of us wakes.

There is no unseeing it. The whites thick
and clotted, erupting into weeds where they fall
near my feet. My people don't share what darkness

we've seen—fear a message from the devil.
Tariq says true dreams reveal themselves at the first
inhale of sunrise. How to hold wide my eyes

for the ineluctable light? On a disappeared horizon
a bush continues to burn, a lilied cervix swarms green,
and Jacob is still sightless, forty years lost to grief.

Clouds drone above me, my two ordinary
eyes sealed in sleep. Every vision is redolent and terrible.
Every temporal sight either a miracle or mistake.

Epistle: Hajar

Agate, alyssum, apricot—simple pleasures
I can still pronounce in this desert.

Love's only dominion, the clear
well-walked path to drinkable water. I hesitate

to ask for answers, remembering the others
forsaken in a basket, garden, well.

There's no one left to write to
but I'd tell of the tree, its sweet shade

at high noon. The untorn snakeskin I found
while digging for wetness in the sand.

Against the crude mountains, his turned back
whittled down by my calls.

I've learned to cull want
from wait,

to walk until water appears.

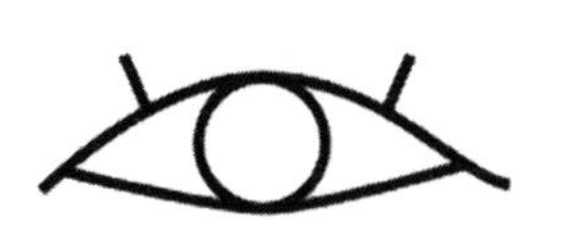

Notes

"Ghazal Ghazal" references "Aaj Jaane Ki Zid Na Karo," an Urdu poem by Fayyaz Hashmi that was popularized when sung by renowned ghazal singer Farida Khanum.

"Litany of al-Bayt" where "bayt" is the transliterated Arabic word for "house," considers the story of how the Kaaba in Mecca, Saudi Arabia was first constructed.

"Tumulus" is after "Confession" by Leila Chatti.

"Daughter" includes a line from "Noctuary" by Lucie Brock-Broido.

"*Le viol*, René Magritte, 1934" is written after Brigit Pegeen Kelly and references a line from Natalie Diaz.

"Apotheosis" is in memory of Noor Muqaddam, 27, who was murdered in Islamabad, Pakistan in 2021 for rejecting a marriage proposal.

"Fatal Music" includes a line from "Ninth Elegy" by Rainer Maria Rilke as translated by David Young.

“When Nabra Hassanen Wakes Up in Jannah” is in memory of Nabra Hassanen, 17, who was murdered in Virginia in 2017. This occurred during the last ten nights of Ramadan, the holiest days of the holiest month for Muslims, when she and her friends were heading to the mosque after getting a late-night meal. The incident is widely considered to be a hate crime, but authorities have called it an act of road rage.

Acknowledgments

A bouquet of gratitude to the editors and staff of the following journals that housed earlier versions of these poems, sometimes with different titles:

128 Lit: "Sarai;" *The Adroit Journal*: "Parable of Flies" (reprinted in *Best New Poets 2022: 50 Poems from Emerging Writers)* & "February Augury" (read by Ada Limón on *The Slowdown* podcast); *The American Poetry Review*: "Apotheosis" (reprinted in *Poetry Daily*); *Bennington Review*: "Litany with Hair;" *The Boiler*: "Annunciation;" *The Chestnut Review*: "Theophanies;" *Electric Literature*: "Roadkill Elegy;" *Faultline*: "Shirk;" *Frontier Poetry:* "Spectacle;" *Hayden's Ferry Review*: "Cicatrix" & "Epistle: Hajar;" *The Journal*: "Self-Portrait as Epiphany;" *The Margins* (AAWW): "Magdalene;" *Memorious*: "Aurat," "Partition Ghazal," & "Self-Portrait as Mouthpiece of God;" *Mizna*: "Litany of al-Bayt;" *Palette Poetry*: "Ghazal Ghazal" & "Ghazal on the Day of;" *Pleiades*: "Mother of Nations;" *Poetry*: "My Faith Gets Grime under Its Nails;" *Quarterly West*: "Daughter Triptych;" *The Rumpus*: "O Gabriel;" *The Seventh Wave*: "Matrilineage [Recovered];" *Slant'd*: "Temporal;" *Tinderbox Poetry Journal*: "Story of the Cranes;" *Verse of April*: "Tumulus;" *Waxwing*: "The Guest;" *wildness*: "Motherhood 1999"

—

All praise is to the Most Merciful, the Most Compassionate—all good is from and through You.

To my teachers: Erick Chase, who made our fifth-grade class write out dictionary definitions when we misbehaved. You meant it as punishment, but it made me a poet. Whitney DeVos, who was my first instructor in poetry and is the reason this book exists. Ronaldo V. Wilson, Rob Sean Wilson, Micah Perks, Dara Barrois/Dixon, Peter Gizzi, Ocean Vuong, Shayla Lawson, Cameron Awkward-Rich, Claire Schwartz, Kaveh Akbar: boundless gratitude. All I know, I've learned from you. To Jennifer Jacobson, whose gifts of warmth and wisdom I hold close. To those who offered the generous words that beckon from the back cover—thank you for helping usher this book into the world.

To the Islamic Scholarship Fund, the University of Massachusetts Amherst MFA for Poets & Writers, the University of California Santa Cruz, the Hambidge Center, the Community of Writers, *The Seventh Wave*, and the Stadler Center for Poetry & Literary Arts at Bucknell University for support at critical junctures.

Boundless gratitude to the incredible people behind Alice James Books: Carey Salerno, Alyssa Neptune, Emily Marquis, Debra Norton, Julia Bouwsma, and Sumita Chakraborty. I am bewilderingly lucky to have found a home for *Theophanies* with you. Thank you to KMA Sullivan and Kary Wayson for your generous feedback early on. Thank you to Dan Hillier, whose breathtaking art graces the cover.

For encouragement, generosity, inspiration, and friendship: Yumna Azizuddin, Hajjar Baban, Gabrielle Bates, Karishma Desai, Summer Farah, Marcella Haddad, Madiha Haque, Malvika Jolly, I. S. Jones, Saba Keramati, Ali-Moosa Mirza, Fatima Farheen Mirza, Joshua Roark, Lubna Safi, Narjis Sheikh, Zainub Tayeb, Chloe Tsolakoglou,

Haolun Xu. Dearest Patrycja Humienik, for a deep well of sistership. So many others who my work and way owe immense gratitude to—thank you.

To my mother, my mother, my mother, and my father, for nurturing a love of reading and writing from a young age.

میں آج جہاں ہوں آپ دونوں کی محبت کی وجہ سے ہوں

To my family, blood and chosen. My brothers, my sisters, my cousins. To all the mothers, known or not, who made me. To T, with every ounce of my love. May we always gaze in the same direction.

Recent Titles from Alice James Books

Orders of Service, Willie Lee Kinard III
The Dead Peasant's Handbook, Brian Turner
The Goodbye World Poem, Brian Turner
The Wild Delight of Wild Things, Brian Turner
I Am the Most Dangerous Thing, Candace Williams
Burning Like Her Own Planet, Vandana Khanna
Standing in the Forest of Being Alive, Katie Farris
Feast, Ina Cariño
Decade of the Brain: Poems, Janine Joseph
American Treasure, Jill McDonough
We Borrowed Gentleness, J. Estanislao Lopez
Brother Sleep, Aldo Amparán
Sugar Work, Katie Marya
Museum of Objects Burned by the Souls in Purgatory, Jeffrey Thomson
Constellation Route, Matthew Olzmann
How to Not Be Afraid of Everything, Jane Wong
Brocken Spectre, Jacques J. Rancourt
No Ruined Stone, Shara McCallum
The Vault, Andrés Cerpa
White Campion, Donald Revell
Last Days, Tamiko Beyer
If This Is the Age We End Discovery, Rosebud Ben-Oni
Pretty Tripwire, Alessandra Lynch
Inheritance, Taylor Johnson
The Voice of Sheila Chandra, Kazim Ali
Arrow, Sumita Chakraborty
Country, Living, Ira Sadoff
Hot with the Bad Things, Lucia LoTempio
Witch, Philip Matthews
Neck of the Woods, Amy Woolard
Little Envelope of Earth Conditions, Cori A. Winrock

Alice James Books is committed to publishing books that matter. The press was founded in 1973 in Boston, Massachusetts to give women access to publishing. As a cooperative, authors performed the day-to-day undertakings of the press. The press continues to expand and grow from its formative roots, guided by its founding values of access, excellence, inclusivity, and collaboration in publishing. Its mission is to publish books that matter and preserve a place of belonging for poets who inspire us. AJB seeks to broaden our collective interpretation of what constitutes the American poetic voice and is dedicated to helping its artists achieve purposeful engagement with broad audiences and communities nationwide. The press was named for Alice James, sister to William and Henry, whose extraordinary gift for writing went unrecognized during her lifetime.

Designed by Pamela A. Consolazio

Spark design

Printed by Sheridan Saline